Written by Julie Douglas • Illustrated by Larry Nolte

Cover design by Gray Communications

Printed in the United States of America by Comfort Printing
10 9 8 7 6 5 4 3 2 1

NAME THOSE NEIGHBORS

California has some interesting neighbors!
An ocean, a foreign country, and three states border California. Can you name them all?

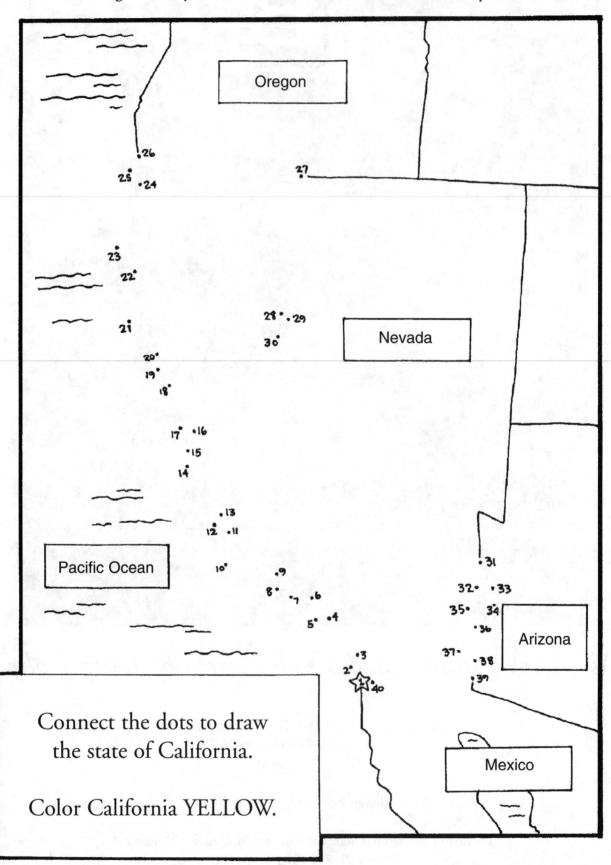

Oregon

•26
25• •24

27•

23•
22•

28• •29
30•

Nevada

21•

20•
19•
18•

17• •16
•15
14•

•13
12• •11

Pacific Ocean

10•

•9
8• •7 •6

5• •4

•31

32• •33
35• 34•
•36

37•
•38
•39

Arizona

•3
2• •40

Connect the dots to draw
the state of California.

Color California YELLOW.

Mexico

ON THE ROAD

Design your own personalized California license plate. You may want to use your name or a nickname and some of your favorite numbers. Then take a "drive" along the highway maze. Watch the speed limit!

What's the weather?

The weather can be very different all over California. Southern California is warm and sunny. Northern California can be cold and rainy. The temperature in the deserts can reach over 100 degrees!

Read the weather reports on the left and draw lines to the clothes and accessories on the right that you would pack if you were traveling to that part of the state.

HINT: You can choose the same article of clothing and/or accessory for more than one weather report.

Sunny today with highs in the 80s.
Breezy and warm.

Cloudy with rain early in the day.
Highs in the 60s.

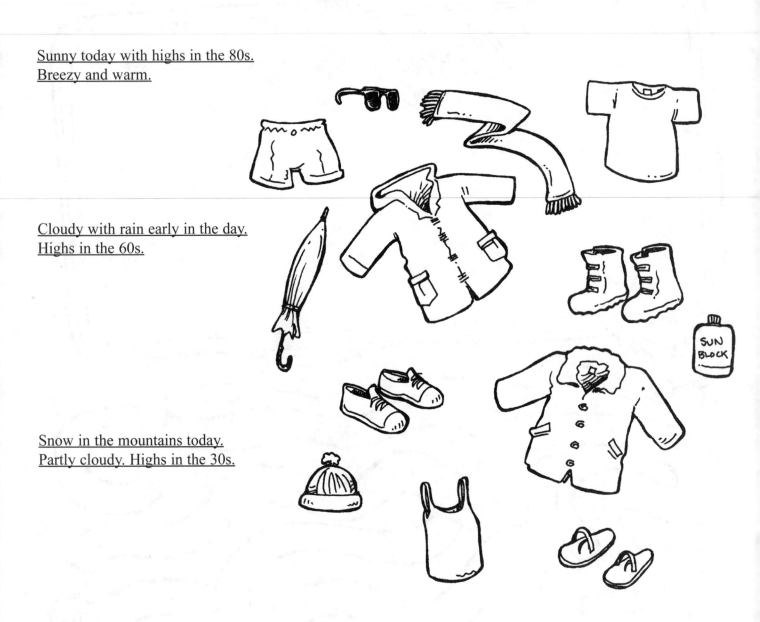

Snow in the mountains today.
Partly cloudy. Highs in the 30s.

Very hot and dry.
Sunny skies with highs in the 90s.

What's to Eat?

A lot of the foods you eat are grown in California. California's weather and rich soil are very helpful to farmers. Can you find some of California's crops in the word search below? The words can be found across, down, and diagonally.

S	T	R	A	W	B	E	R	R	I	E	S	S
C	C	Z	T	P	C	A	H	E	A	M	T	Q
A	E	G	R	A	P	E	S	G	B	U	O	D
R	L	O	C	K	I	N	L	B	N	R	M	A
R	E	C	V	B	S	M	I	L	E	K	A	R
F	R	I	N	N	T	L	A	O	R	O	T	S
L	Y	B	O	I	O	W	F	A	B	Y	O	I
N	Y	M	I	B	Y	A	O	L	I	V	E	S
P	E	L	O	L	I	G	R	A	P	U	S	I
L	C	A	R	R	O	T	S	L	L	D	R	R

WORD LIST

carrots
celery
grapes
lemons
olives
strawberries
tomatoes
walnuts

5

STATE CAPITAL

California became the 31st state in 1850.
The city of Sacramento was chosen as the state capital in 1854.

Connect the dots to draw the California capitol building.

State Flag

Do you know the animal on the California state flag? It is the California Grizzly Bear. The settlers who designed the flag chose the bravest animal that they could think of for their flag. Sadly, the California Grizzly Bear is now extinct.

Color the flag below using the color key.

COLOR KEY

1=Brown   2=Red   3=Green

Stately Colors

The official state colors of California are blue and gold.
Find the hidden picture below. What did you make with the GOLD or YELLOW color?

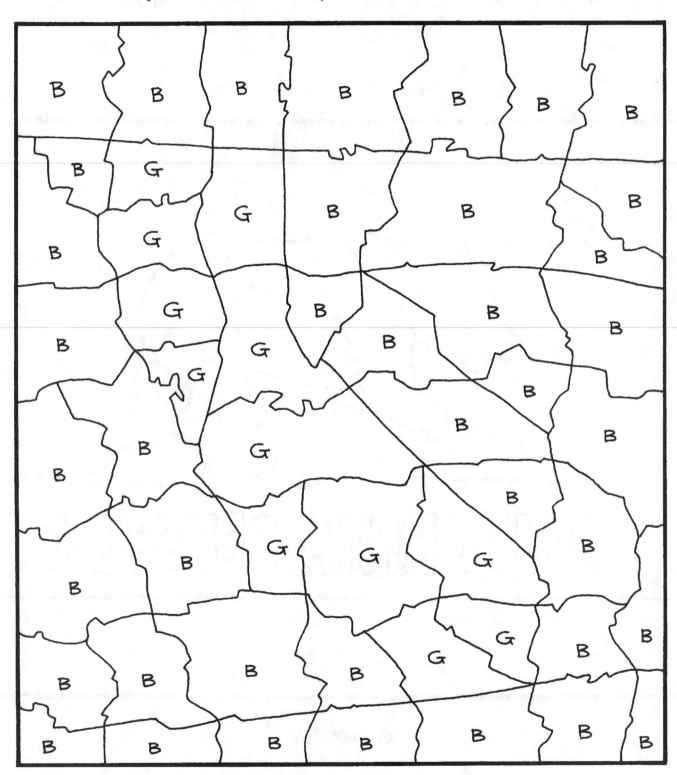

Color those spaces with the letter B BLUE.
Color those spaces with the letter G GOLD or YELLOW.

Great Grapes

California produces more grapes than any other state in the United States. Find seven words associated with grapes in the word search. The words can be found across, down, and diagonally.

```
W   E   J   V   I   N   E   Y   A   R   D   B   R   Y
L   S   U   K   G   L   P   Z   M   A   H   D   W   C
W   H   I   T   E   N   B   B   V   I   J   F   B   A
V   S   C   E   Z   M   L   C   D   S   F   R   U   U
X   O   E   U   K   P   W   Q   H   I   B   L   N   J
Y   T   A   E   M   Z   P   O   N   N   I   K   C   S
H   D   N   F   R   D   K   I   E   S   C   X   H   Q
M   I   B   Z   J   E   L   L   Y   R   Y   P   A   V
V   L   S   O   P   Y   D   F   K   J   B   P   Q   E
```

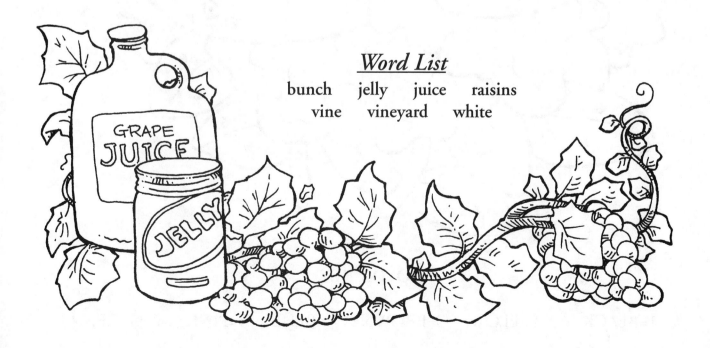

Word List

bunch   jelly   juice   raisins
vine   vineyard   white

9

STATE INSECT

In 1972, Californians named the California Dogface the official state insect.

Use the color key to color the butterfly. Can you see the shape of a dog's head on the wings?

COLOR KEY

1=BLACK   2=YELLOW   3=BROWN   4=BLUE   5=PINK   6=GREEN

State Bird

The California state bird, the California Valley Quail, is a very shy creature.

Can you find the California Valley Quail hiding in this puzzle?
Color all of the spaces marked with a dot BLUE to get a look at the quail.

State Reptile

California was the first state to adopt a state reptile in 1972.
Californians chose the Desert Tortoise. The Desert Tortoise grows to be about one foot long and
weighs 8–10 pounds. Because of its drab coloring, it can hide easily in the desert sand.

Can you find ten hidden tortoises in this desert picture?

STATE FOSSIL

Long ago saber-toothed tigers lived in California. They have been extinct for thousands of years. How do scientists know that saber-toothed tigers lived in California? They have found fossils of the animal in rocks there. The saber-toothed tiger fossil is the state fossil of California.

Connect the dots to see what a saber-toothed tiger may have looked like.

Symbols of California

Can you find the symbols of California? The words can be found across, down, and diagonally. Look for the words in dark print in the word list below.

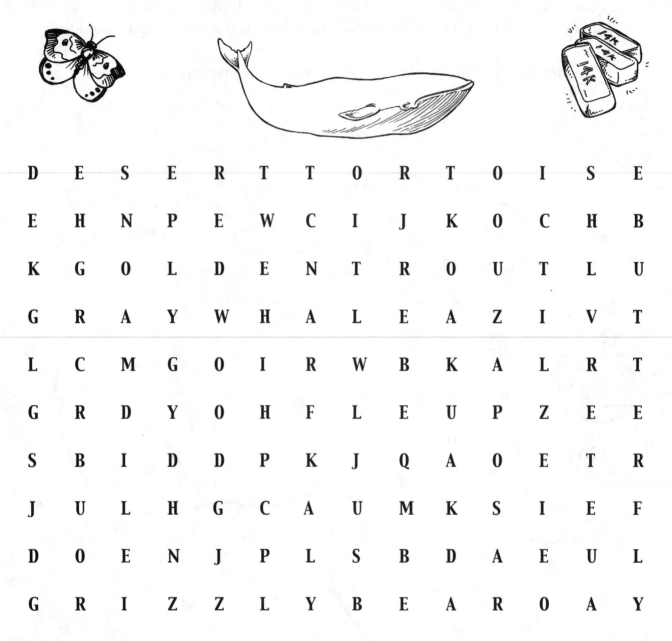

```
D E S E R T T O R T O I S E
E H N P E W C I J K O C H B
K G O L D E N T R O U T L U
G R A Y W H A L E A Z I V T
L C M G O I R W B K A L R T
G R D Y O H F L E U P Z E E
S B I D D P K J Q A O E T R
J U L H G C A U M K S I E F
D O E N J P L S B D A E U L
G R I Z Z L Y B E A R O A Y
```

WORD LIST

State Bird - California Valley **Quail**   State Fish - **Golden Trout**   State Mineral - **Gold**

State Insect - California Dogface **Butterfly**   State Marine Mammal - **Gray Whale**

State Tree - **Redwood**   State Reptile - **Desert Tortoise**   State Mammal - California **Grizzly Bear**

14

CALIFORNIA!

California is a long name!
Each state has an abbreviation, or a short way, to write the name of the state.

Use a BLUE crayon to color each piece of the puzzle below that has the letter C in it.
You will discover the short way to write California.

Spell It

The name "California" was given to the state by Spanish explorers.
It was the name of a make-believe island in a story that they knew.

How many words can you make using the letters in the word **California**? Write your words on the lines.

can _____ _____ _____ _____ _____

_____ _____ _____ _____

_____ _____

_____ _____

CRACK THE CODE

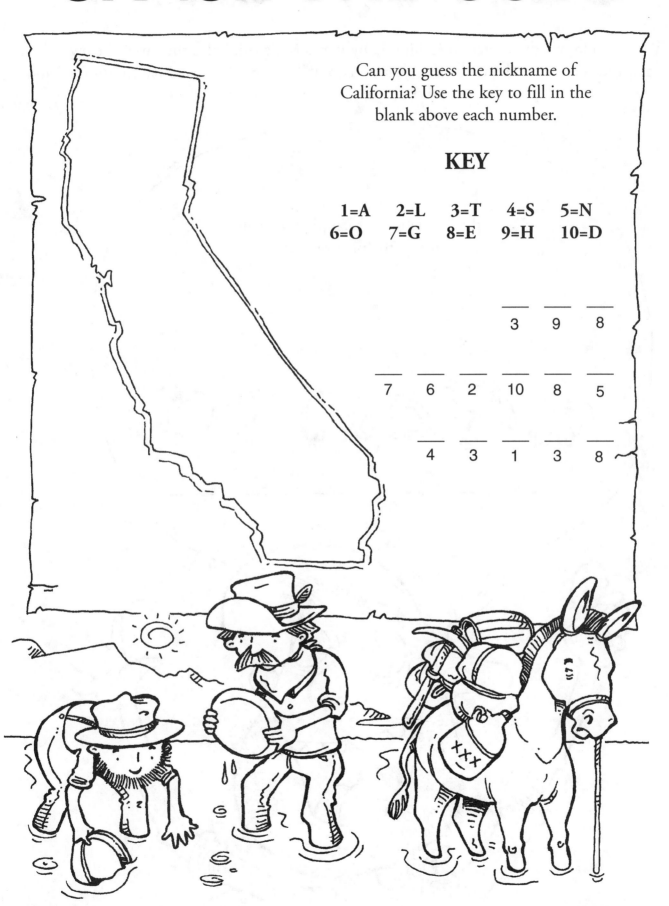

Can you guess the nickname of California? Use the key to fill in the blank above each number.

KEY

1=A	2=L	3=T	4=S	5=N
6=O	7=G	8=E	9=H	10=D

___ ___ ___
3　9　8

___ ___ ___ ___ ___ ___
7　6　2　10　8　5

___ ___ ___ ___ ___
4　3　1　3　8

"I Have Found It!"

In 1848, gold was discovered in California by James Marshall. Solve the puzzle below to find the word that James shouted when he found gold. The word means "I have found it!" and is now the state motto of California.

Write the first letter of each picture's name below the picture.

AN A"MAZE"ING TREE

The largest living tree in the world is in the Sequoia National Forest in California. The tree is called "General Sherman." It is about 272 feet tall. That's as tall as 80 children!

Find your way through the bark maze to reach the top!

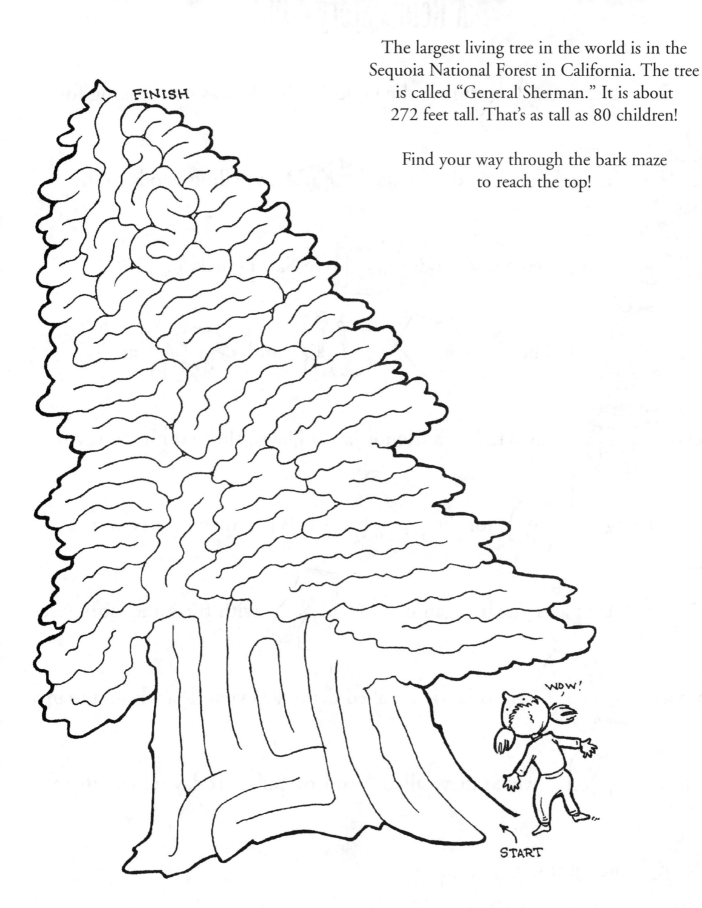

WHO INVENTED BLUE JEANS?
A Rebus Story 4 U!

Levi Strauss came to [California] during the Gold Rush. He was not looking for

[gold nuggets]. Instead, he wanted to make [money] by selling goods to the

[miners]. He opened a dry goods [store] in San Francisco.

The [miners] could buy a [tent], [pick and shovel], and [clothes] at

Levi's [store]. One day Levi's friend, Jacob Davis, showed him a way to

make stronger [pants] for the [miners]. Jacob put metal rivets on the

[pocket]. Levi and Jacob began making [pants] with the same fabric used

to make a [tent]. This fabric is called denim. Levi and Jacob sold many

of these [pants], which they called "waist overalls." Today we call these

[pants] blue jeans.

SURF'S UP DUDE!

Surfing is a totally cool sport. Some of the best surfers in the world go to the beaches of California to enjoy the awesome waves.

Design your own rad surfboard!

Name Game

Have you ever wondered how towns get their names? Some are named for famous people. Others are named for things in nature or history. Many places in California have interesting names.

Can you find some interesting names of California towns in the word search below? The names can be found across, down, and diagonally.

```
H  E  R  C  U  L  E  S  K  A  D  R  G
P  U  M  P  K  I  N  C  E  N  T  E  R
E  Y  N  G  J  W  T  O  B  C  P  R  A
A  H  A  L  F  M  O  O  N  B  A  Y  S
N  E  E  D  L  E  S  L  X  E  R  K  S
U  V  Q  M  D  P  L  U  C  Z  A  I  V
T  S  W  Y  H  B  C  I  N  L  D  G  A
O  R  A  N  G  E  R  A  I  S  I  N  L
F  J  U  S  W  R  D  H  X  Q  S  L  L
R  A  I  N  B  O  W  T  I  V  E  M  E
W  E  E  D  P  A  T  C  H  B  Z  O  Y
```

Word List

Bell   Cool   Grass Valley   Half Moon Bay   Hercules
Needles   Orange   Paradise   Peanut   Pumpkin Center
Rainbow   Raisin   Rice   Weed Patch

Leap Frog

A frog jumping contest is held each year in Calaveras County, California. The contest started when a man named Mark Twain wrote a story about a frog jumping contest.

Find the frog on the right that matches its owner on the left. Connect them with a line.

Lights. Camera. Action!

Have you ever wanted to make a movie? Many of the movies you watch are made in Hollywood. Pretend that you are going to make a movie in Hollywood. Draw some of the characters that will be in your movie. Give your movie a catchy title. Write a sentence or two about your movie.

TAKE ONE: TITLE

the SCRIPT !!

Picture This

Hidden in this picture are some things you might find on a Hollywood movie set.
Put an "X" on them. Look at the words below if you need help.

camera   costume   director's chair   film   lights
microphone   script   video camera

Spooky Places

The Gold Rush of 1849 was a busy time in California. Many people came to strike it rich.
But after a while, the people went back to their homes or moved on to other places.
The towns that they had built were left empty.

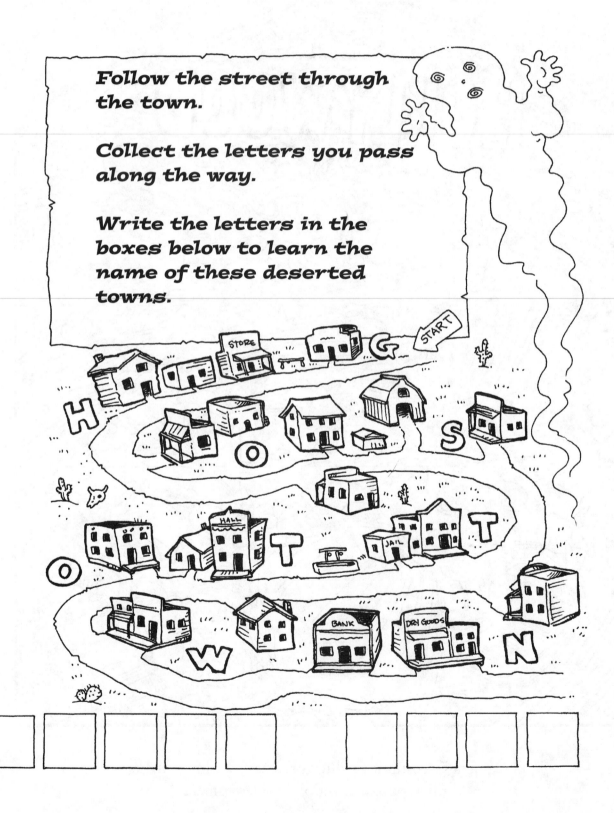

Follow the street through the town.

Collect the letters you pass along the way.

Write the letters in the boxes below to learn the name of these deserted towns.

Get the Picture

Many of Ansel Adams' beautiful photographs of nature were taken in California. Ansel Adams was born in San Francisco in 1902. He was inspired by the beauty of mountains, trees, and deserts. His pictures were usually black and white. Now his photographs are very famous and inspire other photographers.

Can you circle six differences in the two photographs?

Wish You Were Here!

California is a big state with many different kinds of natural places.
Where else could you visit a desert, the mountains, a valley, and the coast all in one state?

Read the postcards and draw a picture for each.

Hi!
We are having fun
driving through a
desert called
Death Valley.
Today we saw a lot
of cacti and a
huge condor.
Wish you were here!

Hi!
The Pacific Ocean is
so beautiful! Today
we built sandcastles
on the beach and
played in the waves.
I liked watching
the surfers.
Wish you were here!

Hi!
The San Joachin
Valley is green and
full of good things to
eat! Today we
stopped at some
farms and tasted
grapes, strawberries,
and broccoli.
Wish you were here!

Hi!
We saw
Mt. Whitney today.
It is the highest
point in the
United States
except for Alaska.
The top was
covered with snow!
We hiked through a
forest, too.
Wish you were here!

For the Birds

Each year in the middle of March, many cliff swallows return to the town of San Juan Capistrano to build their nests. They have been coming here for hundreds of years! The people celebrate the birds' return with festivals and a parade.

Circle the things in the sky that DON'T belong there.

Whales on the Move

Gray whales are the California state marine mammal. A marine mammal spends its life in the water. The gray whales migrate between Alaska and Mexico two times each year. They stop to eat along the coast of California where there are lots of small fish and other sea creatures. Many people like to "whale watch" on the coast of California when the gray whales are on the move.

Can you help the gray whale find its way from Alaska to Mexico? Follow the maze.

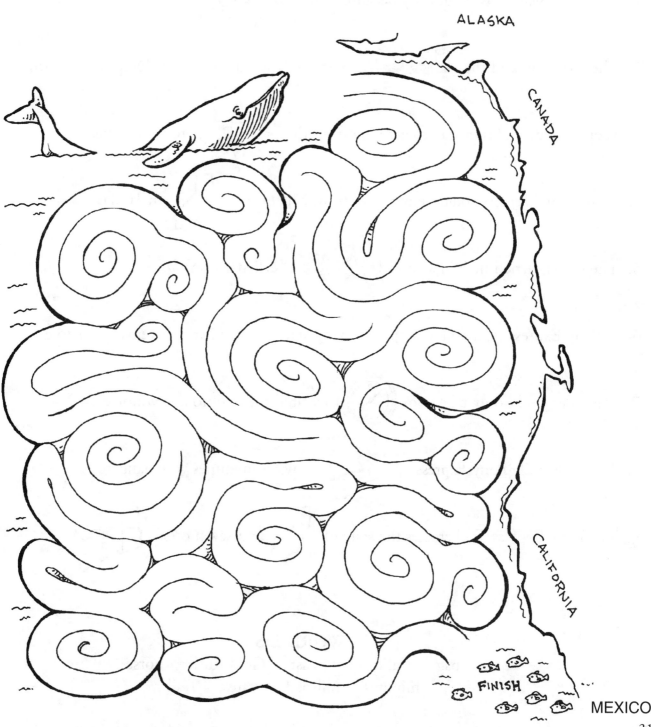

Express Mail

When Californians needed a faster way to send and receive messages with people in the East, the Pony Express was started. Horseback riders carried the mail from St. Joseph, Missouri, to Sacramento, California.

Use the words in the word list below to get the whole story!

1. California was growing quickly because of the  .

2. The telegraph and the  went only as far west as St. Joseph, Missouri.

3. People needed a faster way to get mail from the to California.

4. Pony Express riders could deliver mail from Missouri to in 10 days.

5. The riders carried mail in a special called a *mochila*.

6. A Pony Express rider would stop at a swing station every five to twenty miles to get a

7. The rider could only take two to switch the mail to a new horse.

8. The 2000-mile Pony Express was sometimes very dangerous.

9. The Pony Express Trail crosses the state of and seven other .

WORD LIST

bag   California   east   Gold Rush   horse
minutes   railroad   states   Trail

Special Delivery

The Pony Express riders delivered mail from 1860 to 1861.
The riders crossed wild, unsettled land as fast as they could.

Follow the riders' trails as they cross the wilderness to deliver mail.

Color Pat's trail BLUE.   Color Erin's trail RED.   Color Bessie's trail PURPLE.   Color Steve's trail GREEN.

Fast Food

Do you like hamburgers? Ray Kroc got the idea for McDonald's fast food restaurants after visiting a hamburger stand in San Bernardino. He convinced the owners to let him open more of the little restaurants. Mr. Kroc made a big business selling burgers and shakes!

Look at the picture below and circle seven hamburgers and four milkshakes.

HOME SWEET HOME

Many fancy, brightly painted houses can be found in San Francisco. The name for these kinds of houses is "Victorian-style." But in San Francisco, they are often called "painted ladies."

Decorate and color your own "painted lady" below.

Español

One of California's neighbors is the country of Mexico. In Mexico, the people speak Spanish. Many people in California also speak Spanish.

Look at the pictures below and you can learn some Spanish words, too. The Spanish words are in dark print. Color the pictures.

house...**casa**

car...**carro**

school...**escuela**

bike...**bicicleta**

dog...**perro**

cat...**gato**

book...**libro**

shoes...**zapatos**

pants...**pantalones**

soccer...**fútbol**

flowers...**flores**

birds...**pájaros**

trees...**árboles**

That's Hot!

Spicy, Mexican-style cooking is very popular in California. Do you like to eat foods that are hot?

Look at the pictures of food below. If the food can be hot and spicy, put an "X" on it. If it is not hot and spicy, circle it. Put a star on the food you like the best.

Hello!

San Francisco is home to people from all over the world.
You can hear many different languages being spoken there.

Look below to find out how to say "hello" in different languages.
Draw yourself in the picture and write how you say "hello" in the bubble.

Gung Hay Fat Choy!

Californians in San Francisco's Chinatown celebrate Chinese New Year in early February. They ring in the new year with many old Chinese customs. One of the most exciting is the Golden Dragon Parade. People parade through the streets with large kite-like dragons.

Color the dragon kite below in many bright colors.

Native Americans

Native Americans were the first residents of California. Some of the tribes that lived there were the Pomo, Hupa, Mojave, and Yuma. Many tribes wove baskets from the long, wild grasses that grew in the state. Each tribe created its own basket designs.

You can design your own basket below. Color the squares to make a design on your basket.

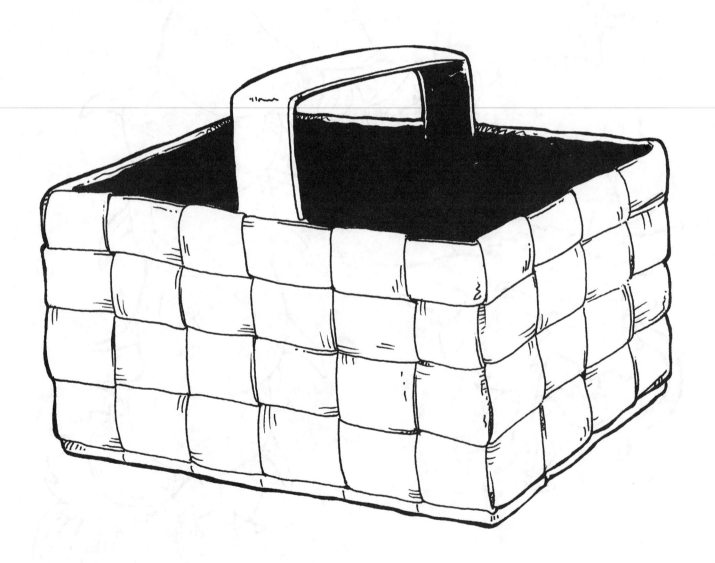

FloJo

Florence Griffith Joyner was born in Los Angeles in 1959. She became a legend in track and field by winning medals in the 1984 and 1988 Olympics. "FloJo" was known for her speed as well as her style. She died in 1998 at the age of 39.

Can you match up the running shoes? Draw a line from each shoe to its mate.

Sports

Californians cheer for many professional sports teams.

Can you match the name of each team with the sport they play?
Draw a line from the name of the team to the equipment that team uses.

Mighty Ducks of Anaheim

Golden State Warriors

LA Dodgers

San Diego Chargers

Oakland Athletics

LA Clippers

Oakland Raiders

Sacramento Kings

San Francisco Giants

Anaheim Angels

San Francisco 49ers

LA Lakers

San Jose Sharks

San Diego Padres

LA Kings

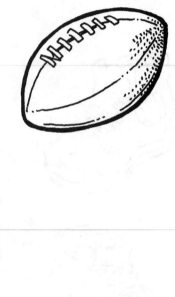

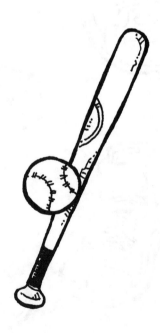

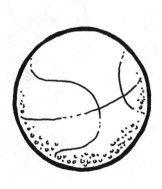

The World's Largest Zoo

Did you know that the largest zoo in the world is in San Diego?

Find the names of some of San Diego's zoo animals in the word search below.
The names can be found across, down, and diagonally.

R H I N O C E R O S E
C C H Y E N A H E A F
G E L K V U L T U R E
O L O C A I N N B N R
R E L V P N M I E E R
I P I A E R G A O W E
L H B O M O W A A B T
L A M G B A A O R I G
A N I O S T R R A O U
L T A R T I G E R L O

WORD LIST

ape elephant ferret gorilla hyena kangaroo
llama newt rhinoceros tiger vulture

WILD THINGS

Many wild animals live in California.

Look at the picture of each animal and unscramble the letters to spell the animal's name.

lhawe __ __ __ __ __

lke __ __ __

asel __ __ __ __

edre __ __ __ __

xfo __ __ __

tyoceo __ __ __ __ __ __

gelae __ __ __ __ __

drlazi __ __ __ __ __ __

44

California Condor

The largest bird in North America lives in the deserts of California. This huge bird is called the California Condor. Its wingspan can be over 9 feet. Wingspan means from the tip of one wing to the tip of the other. You can measure your own "wingspan" by spreading your arms out to your sides and measuring from the tip of your left hand to the tip of your right hand.

Connect the dots to draw a picture of this giant, but endangered, bird.
Start with A and end with XX.

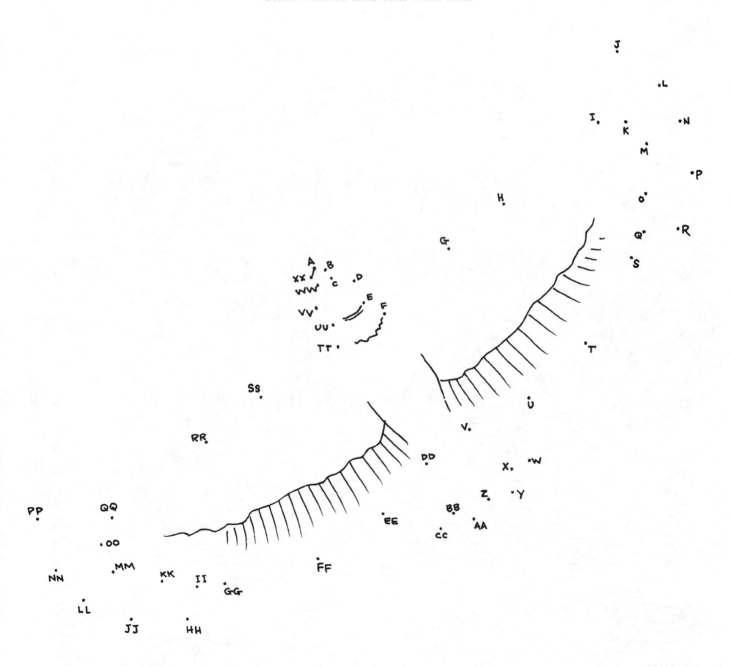

Sunken Treasure

The La Brea Tarpits are full of treasures...fossils! Scientists think that animals came to drink in the marshy area long ago. They became trapped in the tar below the water. Many years later their bones were found. Scientists can learn about the kinds of animals that lived in California by studying fossils. They can then draw pictures of what they think the animals might have looked like.

Look at the picture below and circle the hidden objects.
Can you find a fish, wooly mammoth, sloth, bison, and a seashell?

World's Oldest Tree

Scientists think that a tree in California is over 4,600 years old! That would make it the oldest living tree in the world. This bristlecone pine tree lives in the White Mountains in California.

Use the picture code to find the nickname of this old tree.
Write the first letter of each picture in the space below. The letters will spell the answer.

‾‾‾‾ ‾‾‾‾ ‾‾‾‾ ‾‾‾‾ ‾‾‾‾ ‾‾‾‾ ‾‾‾‾ ‾‾‾‾ ‾‾‾‾ ‾‾‾‾

Toys!

Did you know that the inventors of the Barbie and Ken dolls were Californians?
Ruth and Elliot Handler designed the famous dolls and named them after their own children.

What kind of a toy would you like to invent? Use your imagination to draw a brand new toy using the shapes below. What will you call your new toy?

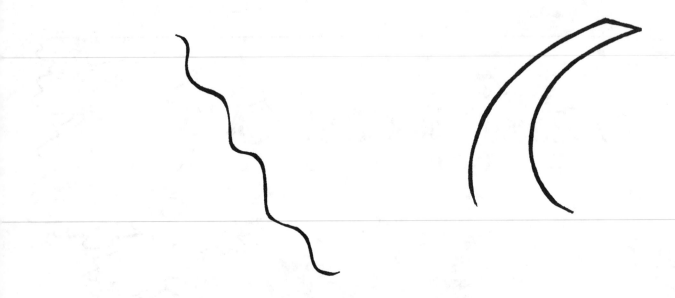

INVENTORS

Do you like computers? The men who built the first Apple Computer were Californians. Stephen Wozniak and Steven Jobs designed a computer that would be easy enough for people to use in their own homes.

Think of an activity that you like to do using a computer. Draw it on the computer screen.

Out of This World

Scientists use the huge Hale telescope at the Palomar Observatory in California to study outer space. The Hale telescope lets them see comets, asteroids, stars, and planets.

Can you find ten things that scientists would NOT see in the sky? Circle them.

First U.S. Woman in Space

Did you know the first American woman to fly in space was born and raised in California? Sally Ride took her famous flight on board the *Challenger* in 1983. She went into space again in 1984. After working as an astronaut, Sally became a teacher at a university in California.

Look at the space shuttles below. Can you find the two that are exactly the same?

Waterfall

The highest waterfall in the United States can be found in Yosemite National Park in California.

Collect all of the capital letters as they tumble over the falls.

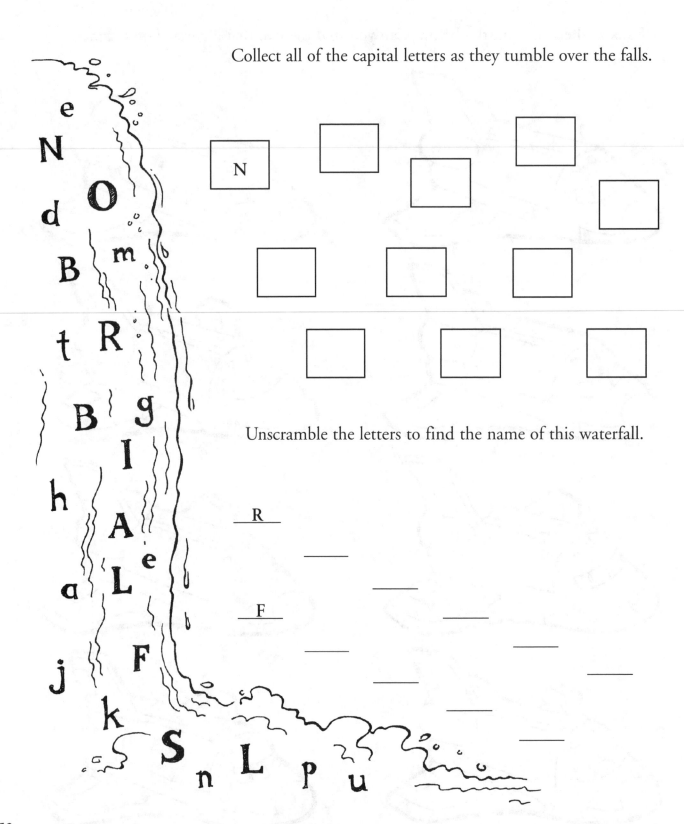

Unscramble the letters to find the name of this waterfall.

R ___

___ ___

F ___ ___ ___

___ ___

___

Disneyland

Do you like the movies made by Walt Disney?
In California, visitors enjoy rides and shows at an amusement park called Disneyland.

Follow the roller coaster ride to learn the name of the mouse who made Walt Disney famous.
Start with "M" and write every other letter in the boxes below.

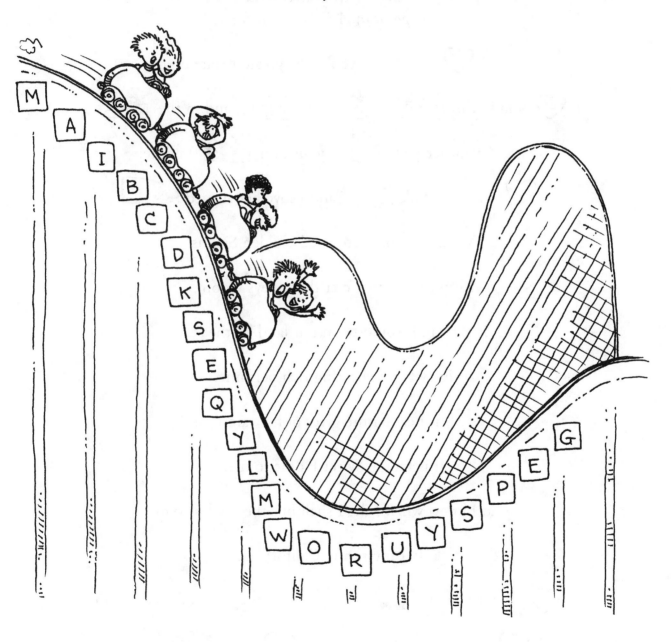

___ ___ ___ ___ ___ ___ ___ ___ ___ ___ ___ ___

Something to Sing About!

Californians love their state!
Read the words to their state song. Look at the picture clues for help.

I Love You, California
written by F.B. Silverwood
composed by A.F. Frankenstein

I ♡ you, [California], you're the greatest state of all.

I ♡ you in the [winter], [summer], [spring], and in the [fall].

I ♡ your fertile [valleys]: your dear [mountains] I adore,

I ♡ your grand old [ocean] and I love her rugged [shore].

When the snow crowned Golden Sierras

Keep their watch o'er the valleys bloom.

It is there I would be in our land by the sea,

Ev'ry breeze bearing rich perfume,

It is here nature gives of her rarest,

It is Home Sweet Home to me.

And I know when I die I shall breathe my last sigh

For my sunny California.

I ♡ your redwood [forest] — ♡ your [field] of yellow grain,

I ♡ your [summer] breezes, and I ♡ your [winter] rain,

I ♡ you, land of [flowers]; land of [honey], [grapes] and wine.

I ♡ you, [California]; you have won this heart of mine.

Match It Up!

Now draw a line between the picture clue on the left and its word on the right.

  Winter

  Spring

  Fall

  Summer

  Forests

  California

  Fields

  Shore

  Love

  Valleys

  Mountains

  Ocean

  Flowers

  Honey

  Fruit

What's Its Name?

This bridge in San Francisco is HUGE. At first, people thought a bridge this large couldn't be built. But the bridge was finished in 1937. It is over 4,000 feet long. It has a tower that is over 700 feet tall! The bridge is painted a color called International Orange.

Write the name of each picture on the line below it to find out the name of this famous bridge.

_____   _____

_____

A "POPULAR" STATE

California has more of something than any other state.

Read the riddle below. Can you solve it? Use the code to find the answer.

CLUES:
1. They come in many shapes, sizes, and colors.
2. Your see them every day.
3. You are one of these.

SECRET CODE:
Each face stands for a different letter. Use the code to spell the answer to the riddle.

A P L J O E R S D M

___ ___ ___ ___ ___ ___

Play Time!

Lake Tahoe is a fun place to play.

Find the many different things that visitors can do at Lake Tahoe in the word search below.
The words can be found across, down, and diagonally.

WORD LIST

bike

camp

golf

hike

kayak

sail

ski

swim

S	W	I	M	U	N	E	R	U	S	B
C	C	W	K	U	V	A	H	E	A	F
G	B	L	K	A	Y	A	K	U	R	E
C	L	O	C	E	I	G	O	L	F	B
A	E	L	K	P	N	E	I	E	E	I
M	P	I	A	E	K	G	A	O	W	K
P	S	B	O	I	I	Z	A	A	B	E
L	A	M	H	H	A	A	O	S	I	G
A	I	I	O	S	T	Z	R	A	K	U
L	L	A	K	A	Y	G	E	R	L	I

ANSWER KEY

Page 2:

The Pacific Ocean is California's bordering ocean.

Mexico is its bordering country.

Oregon, Nevada, and Arizona are California's three neighboring states.

Page 3:

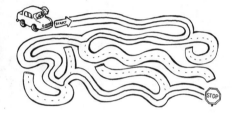

Page 4:

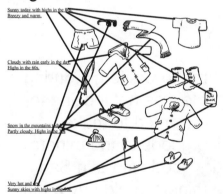

Page 5:

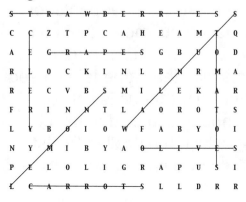

Page 6:

Page 8:
California

Page 9:

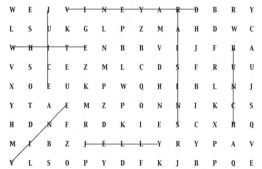

Page 11:

Page 12:

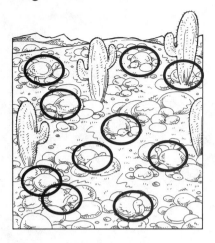

Page 13:

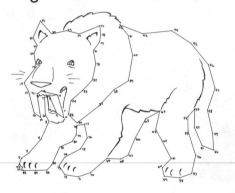

Page 14:

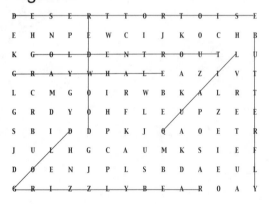

Page 15:

Page 16:
Answers will vary. Some words from California: can, corn, an, calf, coin, in, loan, air, on, of, if, for, fan, fin, foal, con, coil, foil, coal, ran, fair, lain, rain, rail, nail, frail.

Page 17:
The Golden State

Page 18:
Eureka

Page 19:

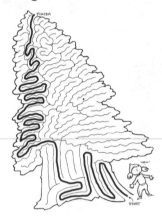

Page 20:
Levi Strauss came to California during the Gold Rush. He was not looking for gold. Instead, he wanted to make money by selling goods to the miners. He opened a dry goods store in San Francisco. The miners could buy a tent, tools, and clothes at Levi's store. One day Levi's friend, Jacob Davis, showed him a way to make stronger pants for the miners. Jacob put metal rivets on the pockets. Levi and Jacob began making pants with the same fabric used to make a tent. This fabric is called denim. Levi and Jacob sold many of these pants, which they called "waist overalls." Today we call these pants blue jeans.

Page 22:

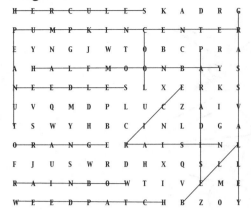

Page 23:

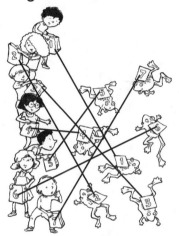

Page 25:

Page 26:
Ghost town

Page 27:

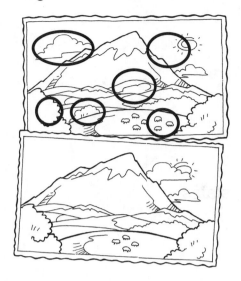

Page 30:

Page 31:

Page 32:
1. Gold Rush
2. railroad
3. east
4. California
5. bag
6. horse
7. minutes
8. Trail
9. California, states

Page 34:

Page 37:

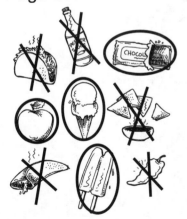

Page 41:

Page 42:

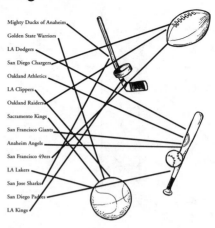

Page 43:

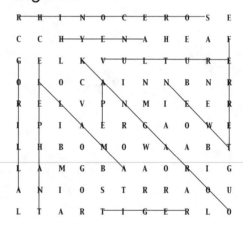

Page 44:
1. whale
2. elk
3. seal
4. deer
5. fox
6. coyote
7. eagle
8. lizard

Page 45:

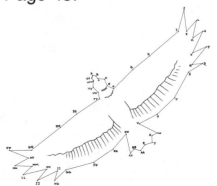

Page 46:

Page 47:
Methuselah

Page 50:

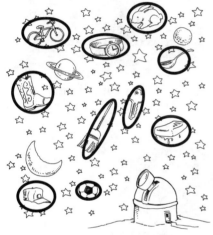

Page 51:

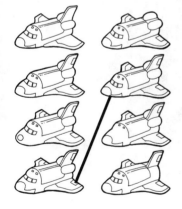

Page 52:
Ribbon Falls

Page 53:
Mickey Mouse

Page 54:
I love you California, you're the greatest state of all. I love you in the winter, summer, spring, and in the fall. I love your fertile valleys: your dear mountains I adore, I love your grand old ocean and I love her rugged shore. When the snow crowned Golden Sierras Keep their watch o'er the valleys bloom. It is there I would be in our land by the sea, Ev'ry breeze bearing rich perfume, It is here nature gives of her rarest, It is Home Sweet Home to me. And I know when I die I shall breathe my last sigh For my sunny California. I love your redwood forests — love your fields of yellow grain, I love your summer breezes, and I love your winter rain, I love you, land of flowers; land of honey, fruit and wine. I love you, California; you have won this heart of mine.

Page 55:

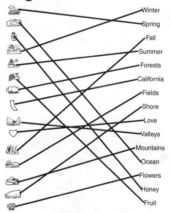

Page 56:
Golden Gate Bridge

Page 57:
People

Page 58:

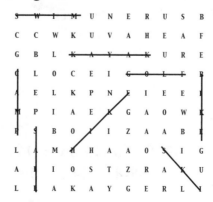

Take off with the *Alpha Flight Books* Series!

Here's a series of hardcover jacketed ABC books that will teach children the alphabet while also giving them interesting information about each letter's topic. The series is designed for the preschool and beginning reader, but its format and fun facts make it suitable for ages 4-8. Each letter of the alphabet will have a two-page spread consisting of:
•the letter in both upper and lower case   •a three to four sentence explanation of each letter's topic
•a photograph   •illustrations

"C" is for California
1892920271 • $17.95

"C" is for Canada
1892920301 • $17.95

"M" is for Missouri
1892920263 • $17.95

**"M" is for Missouri's
Rocks and Minerals**
1892920298 • $17.95

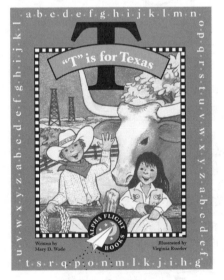

"T" is for Texas
189292028X • $17.95

GHB Publishers

3906 Old Highway 94 South, Suite 300 / St. Charles, Missouri 63304
888-883-4427 / FAX: 636-441-7941 / www.ghbpublishers.com